SNAKES ALIVE

Tiger Snakes

by Ellen Frazel

BLASTOFF!
READERS
3

BELLWETHER MEDIA • MINNEAPOLIS, MN

Note to Librarians, Teachers, and Parents:

Blastoff! Readers are carefully developed by literacy experts and combine standards-based content with developmentally appropriate text.

Level 1 provides the most support through repetition of high-frequency words, light text, predictable sentence patterns, and strong visual support.

Level 2 offers early readers a bit more challenge through varied simple sentences, increased text load, and less repetition of high-frequency words.

Level 3 advances early-fluent readers toward fluency through increased text and concept load, less reliance on visuals, longer sentences, and more literary language.

Level 4 builds reading stamina by providing more text per page, increased use of punctuation, greater variation in sentence patterns, and increasingly challenging vocabulary.

Level 5 encourages children to move from "learning to read" to "reading to learn" by providing even more text, varied writing styles, and less familiar topics.

Whichever book is right for your reader, Blastoff! Readers are the perfect books to build confidence and encourage a love of reading that will last a lifetime!

This edition first published in 2012 by Bellwether Media, Inc.

No part of this publication may be reproduced in whole or in part without written permission of the publisher. For information regarding permission, write to Bellwether Media, Inc., Attention: Permissions Department, 5357 Penn Avenue South, Minneapolis, MN 55419.

Library of Congress Cataloging-in-Publication Data

Frazel, Ellen.
  Tiger snakes / by Ellen Frazel.
    p. cm. – (Blastoff! readers. Snakes alive)
  Includes bibliographical references and index.
  Summary: "Simple text and full-color photography introduce beginning readers to tiger snakes. Developed by literacy experts for students in kindergarten through third grade"–Provided by publisher.
  ISBN 978-1-60014-615-2 (hardcover : alk. paper)
  1. Tiger snakes–Juvenile literature. I. Title.
  QL666.O64F736 2011
  597.96'4–dc22
                                            2011004209

Printed in the United States of America, North Mankato, MN.
080111   1187

Contents

Tiger snakes are large, **poisonous** snakes. They are named for the stripes that cover their bodies.

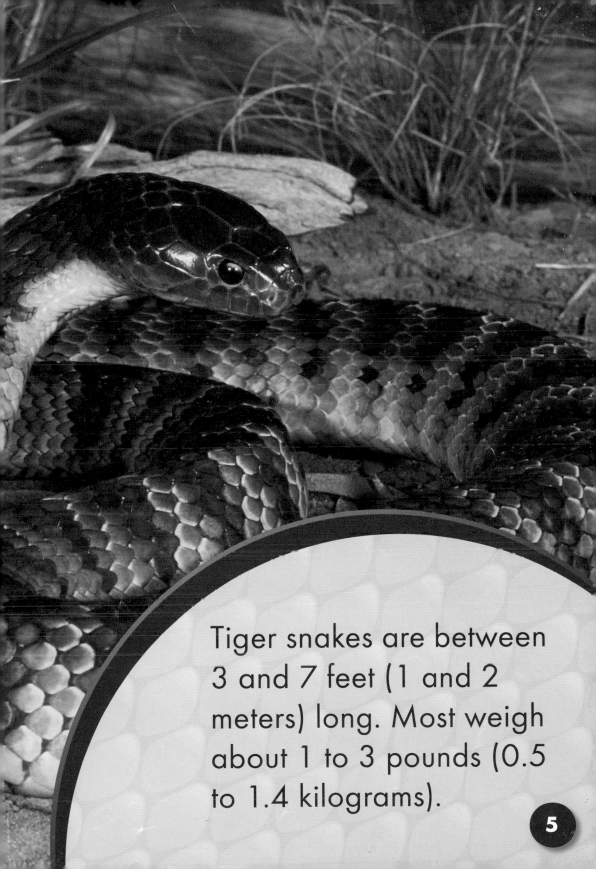

Tiger snakes are between 3 and 7 feet (1 and 2 meters) long. Most weigh about 1 to 3 pounds (0.5 to 1.4 kilograms).

Tiger snakes have **scales** on their bodies. Most have yellow, orange, or green-gray stripes. Some tiger snakes are all black or brown.

The scales on their bellies are called **scutes**. Tiger snakes pull on their scutes with strong muscles to move forward.

scutes

= areas where tiger snakes live

Tiger snakes live in southern Australia, Tasmania, and on nearby islands.

They make homes in **wetlands** and grasslands.

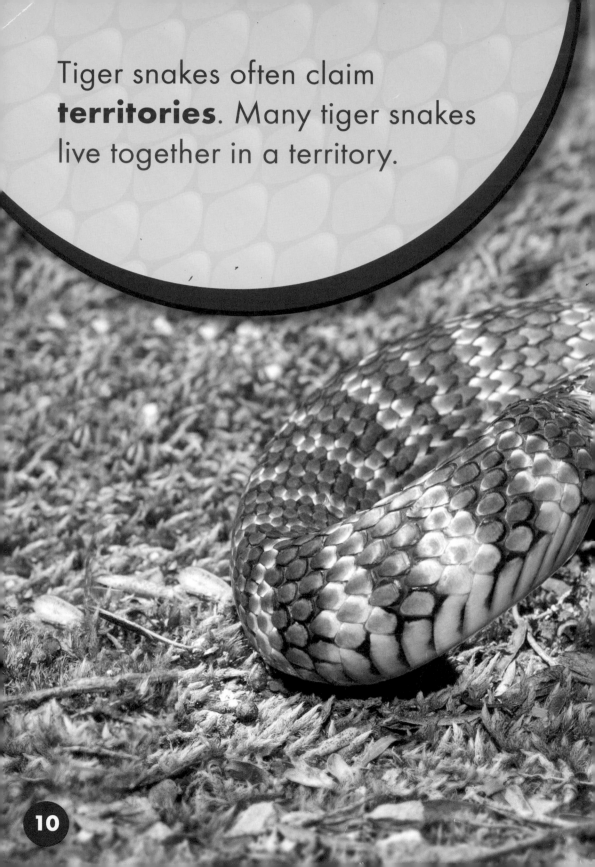

Tiger snakes often claim **territories**. Many tiger snakes live together in a territory.

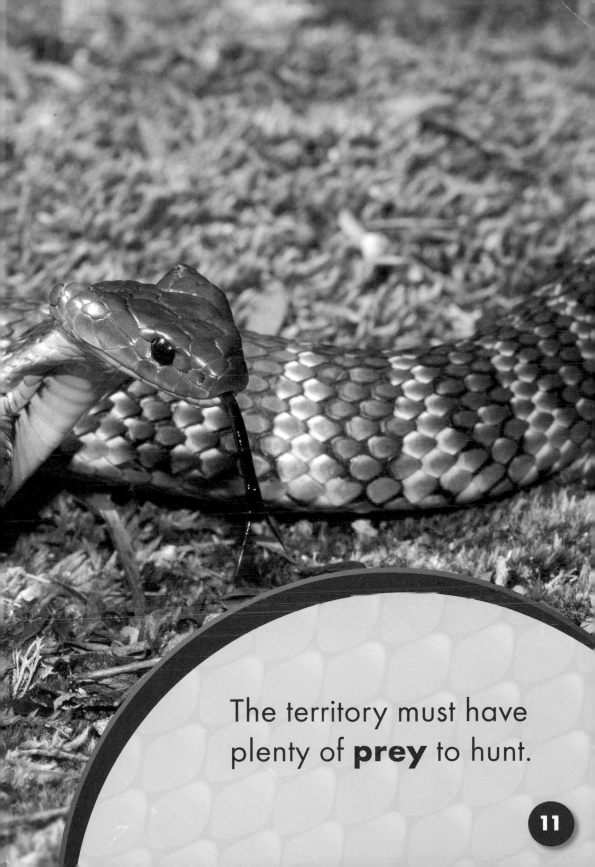

The territory must have plenty of **prey** to hunt.

tiger snake prey

Tiger snakes use forked tongues to smell for prey. They hunt frogs, lizards, birds, and other animals.

Tiger snakes also climb trees to steal eggs from bird nests.

Tiger snakes hunt during the day. Their colors and stripes act as **camouflage**.

14

They help tiger
snakes hide
and sneak up
on their prey.

15

A tiger snake sinks its **fangs** into its prey. **Venom** travels through the hollow fangs and kills the prey.

Then the tiger snake opens its jaws.
It swallows the animal whole!

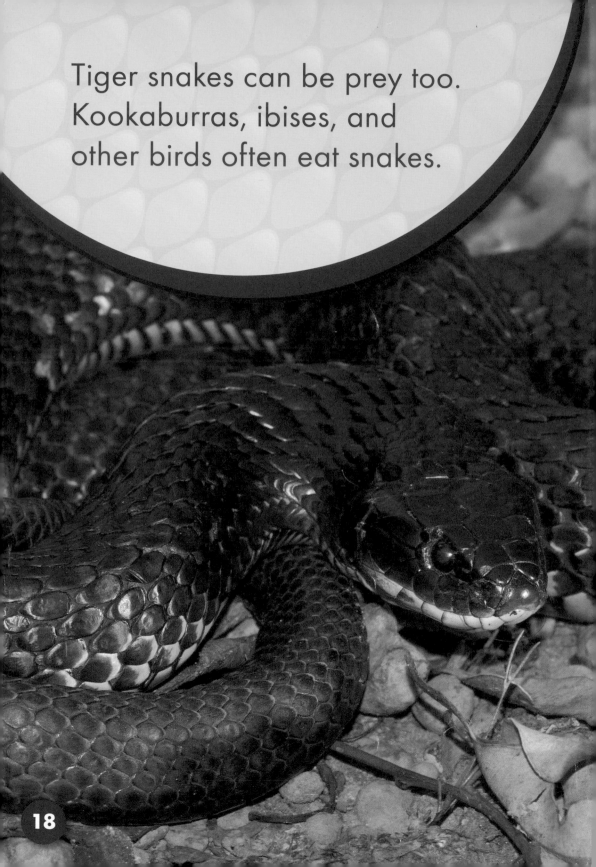

Tiger snakes can be prey too. Kookaburras, ibises, and other birds often eat snakes.

kookaburra

Other poisonous
snakes also hunt
tiger snakes.

A tiger snake raises its body into the air to face a **predator**. It hisses and shows its fangs.

The tiger snake flattens the top part of its body. It **strikes** before the predator can attack!

21

Glossary

camouflage—coloring and patterns that hide an animal by making it look like its surroundings

fangs—sharp, curved teeth; tiger snakes have hollow fangs through which venom can move into a bite.

poisonous—able to kill or harm with a poison; the venom that tiger snakes make is a poison.

predator—an animal that hunts other animals for food

prey—animals hunted by other animals for food

scales—small plates of skin that cover and protect a snake's body

scutes—large scales on the belly of a snake that are attached to muscles; snakes use scutes to move from place to place.

strikes—quickly throws the head and front part of the body at a predator or prey

territories—areas where animals live and hunt; tiger snakes live together in territories.

venom—a poison that some snakes make; tiger snake venom is deadly.

wetlands—wet, spongy land; bogs, marshes, and swamps are wetlands.

To Learn More

AT THE LIBRARY

Jackson, Tom. *Deadly Snakes*. New York, N.Y.:
Gareth Stevens Pub., 2011.

Parish, Steve. *Australian Snakes*. Brisbane, Australia:
Steve Parish Publishing, 2006.

Whittley, Sarah. *Snakes*. New York, N.Y.: St. Martin's
Press, 2002.

ON THE WEB

Learning more about tiger snakes
is as easy as 1, 2, 3.

1. Go to www.factsurfer.com.

2. Enter "tiger snakes" into the search box.

3. Click the "Surf" button and you will see a list of
   related Web sites.

With factsurfer.com, finding more information is just a
click away.

Index